I0797364

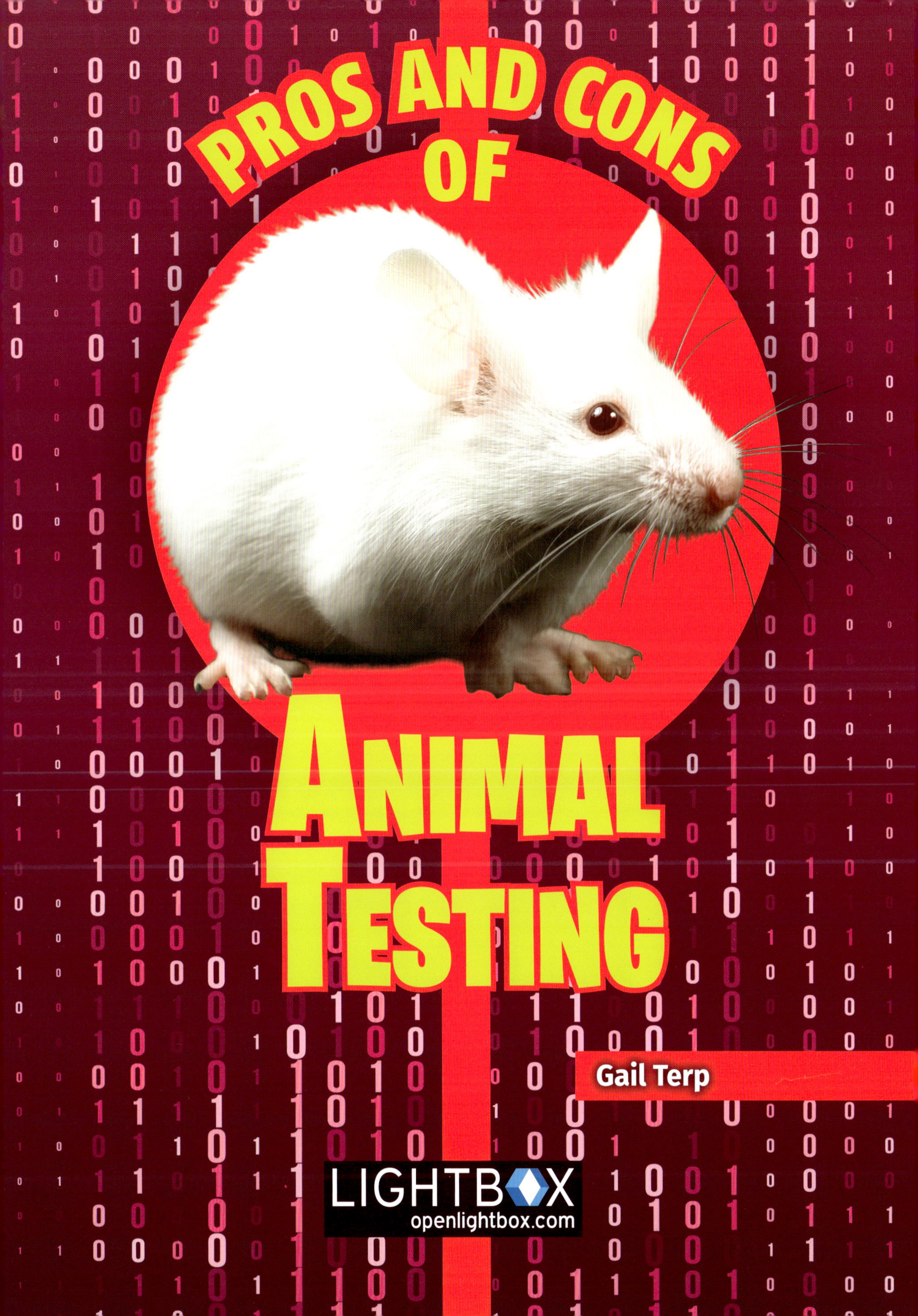
PROS AND CONS OF
ANIMAL TESTING
Gail Terp
LIGHTBOX
openlightbox.com

Go to
www.openlightbox.com
and enter this book's
unique code.

ACCESS CODE

L B X N 3 2 4 9

Lightbox is an all-inclusive digital solution for the teaching and learning of curriculum topics in an original, groundbreaking way. Lightbox is based on National Curriculum Standards.

STANDARD FEATURES OF LIGHTBOX

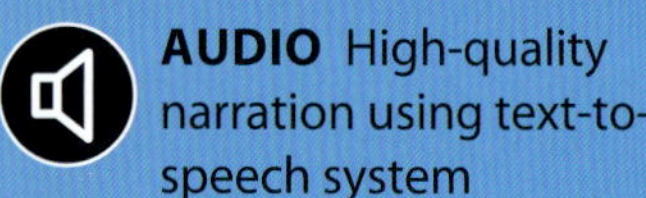
AUDIO High-quality narration using text-to-speech system

ACTIVITIES Printable PDFs that can be emailed and graded

SLIDESHOWS Pictorial overviews of key concepts

VIDEOS Embedded high-definition video clips

WEBLINKS Curated links to external, child-safe resources

TRANSPARENCIES Step-by-step layering of maps, diagrams, charts, and timelines

INTERACTIVE MAPS Interactive maps and aerial satellite imagery

QUIZZES Ten multiple choice questions that are automatically graded and emailed for teacher assessment

KEY WORDS Matching key concepts to their definitions

Contents

Studying animals such as mice helps researchers discover ways to treat and prevent diseases.

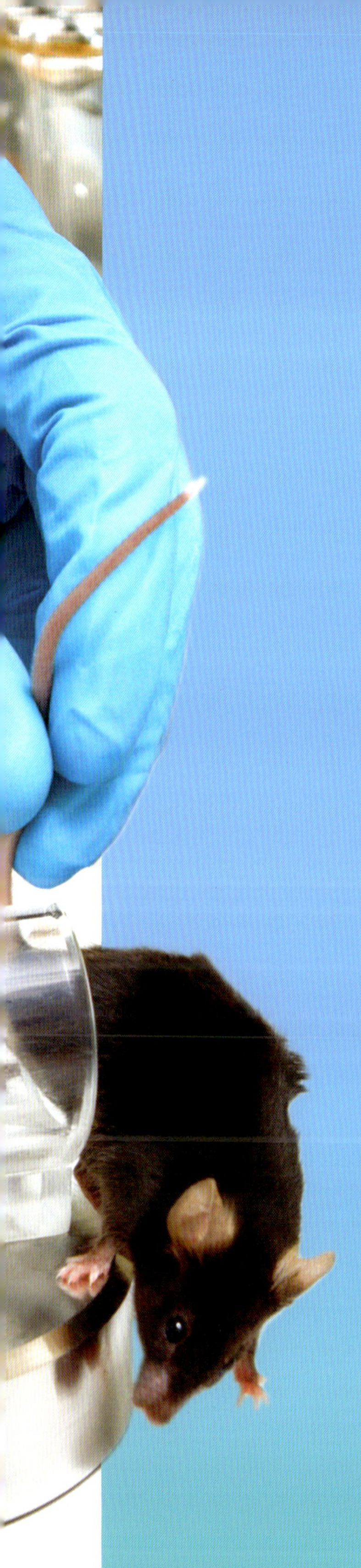

Introduction to Animal Testing

Doctors and veterinarians strive to improve the health of their patients. They work to prevent and cure illness. Many illnesses cause exhaustion and severe pain. These **symptoms** can make it difficult to work or feel pleasure. Treating illness is often expensive. But if left untreated, illnesses may cause additional suffering or even death. To learn of the best treatments, doctors often turn to medical research.

One way that scientists research illness is by using animals. Animals make good research subjects because they are so similar to humans. Rats, mice, fish, and birds make up the largest research group. These animals are used for 90 to 95 percent of the animal research in the United States. But research labs use many types of animals. They use cats, dogs, rabbits, guinea pigs, and hamsters. Labs also use farm animals such as sheep and pigs. Some labs use primates such as monkeys and chimpanzees.

Many medical breakthroughs have occurred because of animal testing. But not everyone agrees that animals should be used for testing. The methods used in the tests can harm the animals. In some cases, the tests do not provide reliable information. For these reasons, opponents of animal testing believe that medical researchers should use other methods instead. The debate about this complicated issue will likely continue for many years to come.

Animals Used for Research

Research labs in the United States used the following animals in 2016. Because labs only report animals covered by the Animal Welfare Act, these statistics do not include most mice, rats, and fish.

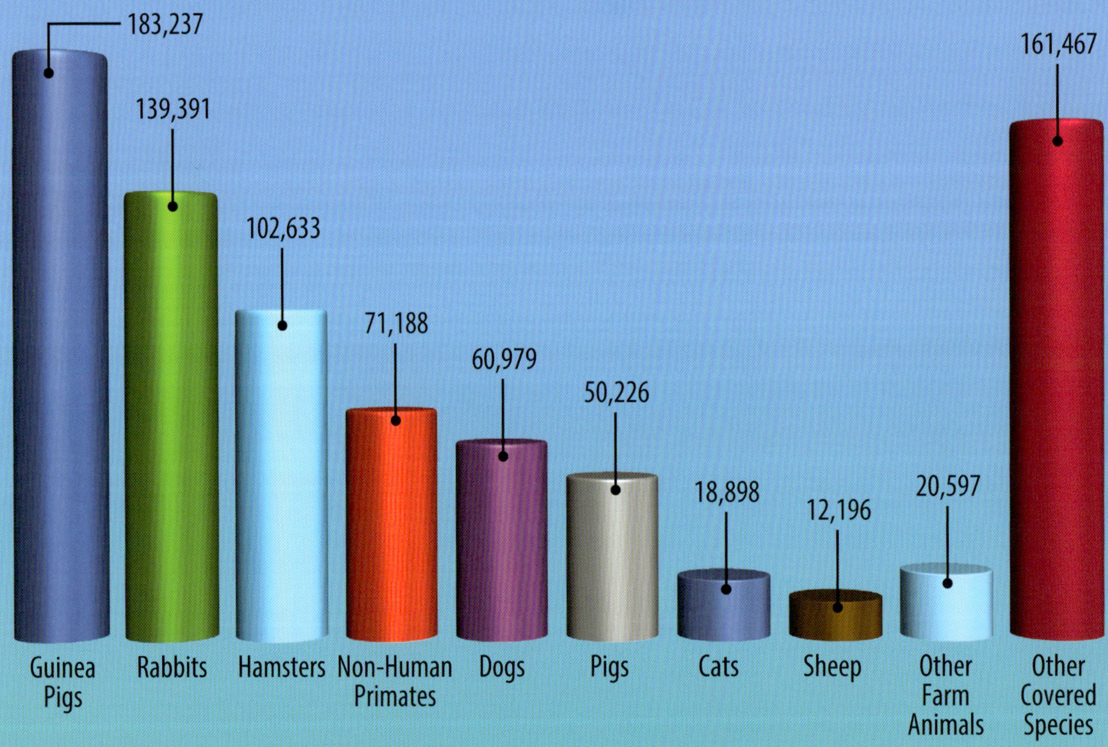

Timeline

1904 Russian physiologist Ivan Petrovich Pavlov is awarded the Nobel Prize in Physiology or Medicine for his work using animals to understand digestion.

1938 The United States Food, Drug and Cosmetic Act becomes law. This requires that cosmetics and drugs be tested to ensure their safety.

1959 In their book, *The Principles of Humane Experimental Technique*, William Russell and Rex Burch create guidelines known as the Three Rs of animal testing.

1966 The Animal Welfare Act becomes law, setting care requirements for animals. However, many common test animals are not included in the law.

2000 The Interagency Coordination Committee on the Validation of Alternative Methods (ICCVAM) is established to research alternatives to animal testing.

2018 California becomes the first U.S. state to ban cosmetics that are tested on animals. This law will take effect on January 1, 2020.

Research with animals helped scientists learn how to manage diabetes.

PRO

Animal Testing Leads to Medical Breakthroughs

Animal testing has led to many important medical discoveries. Diseases that once caused great suffering and even death can now be treated. For example, research with dogs in the 1920s helped scientists find a treatment for diabetes. When people have diabetes, their bodies cannot regulate **glucose**. In addition to causing fatigue, this disease can lead to kidney or nerve damage.

Animal testing helped researchers learn that diabetes affects an organ called the pancreas. In 1921, researchers did surgery to remove this organ from several dogs. After the surgery, the dogs developed diabetes. The researchers discovered that the pancreas produces a chemical called insulin. Insulin controls and adjusts the body's use of sugars and starches. When researchers gave the dogs injections of insulin, the dogs' diabetes improved.

The researchers realized that diabetes occurs when the body does not produce enough insulin. In 1922, the first person received an insulin injection. This treatment was successful. Soon, insulin was used to help many people.

Research with animals also helped scientists understand heart disease. This serious disease can lead to heart attacks or death. But scientists have found several ways to treat heart disease. One treatment is a pacemaker. This device is placed inside a person's chest. It helps control the person's heartbeat. The first pacemakers were created in the 1950s based on research with dogs.

Did You Know?

In the past decade, research with mice has led to surgery that improves vision in people who are blind.

Heart **transplants** are another way to treat heart disease. Doctors performed the first human heart transplant in 1967. Research with dogs also helped make this important achievement possible.

Hypertension often leads to heart disease. Testing with rats or primates helps researchers find ways to treat this condition. Researchers in the 2000s found that baboons and humans can have the same kind of hypertension. Studying baboons may help researchers understand which **genes** cause this problem.

Today, pacemakers are about the same size as a large coin.

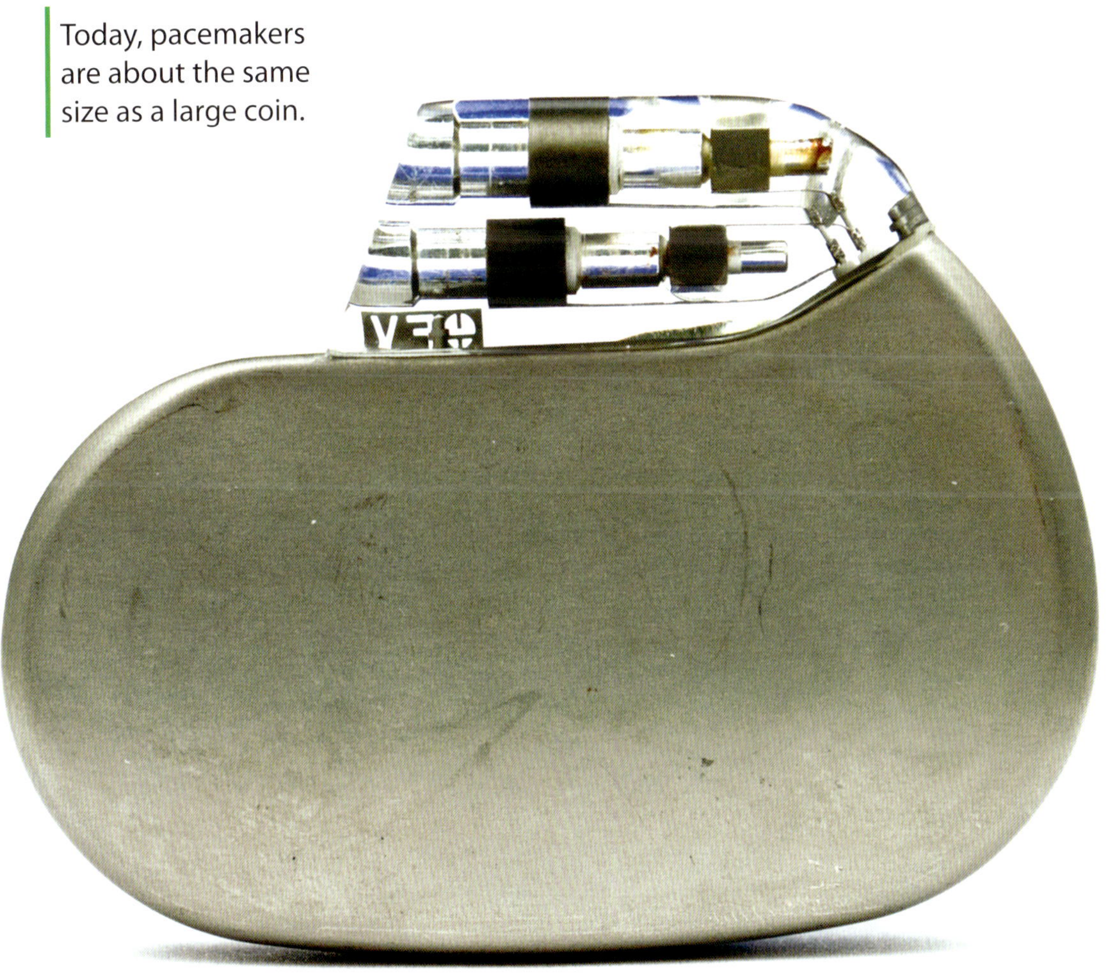

Mice can be used to study heart disease, seizures, and the immune system.

The cancer survival rate in the United States has doubled since the 1970s. This is largely due to animal research. Researchers use mice to learn about leukemia. In this form of cancer, the body forms too many white blood cells. Studying mice that have leukemia helps researchers create new drugs and treatments for the disease.

Animal testing may lead to new treatments for other diseases as well. For instance, Alzheimer's is a brain disease that causes memory loss. Scientists are studying animals to look for a cure. Current research with sea snails may reveal how and where brains store memories.

The majority of people suffering from Alzheimer's are **age 65** or older.

In **2017**, providing care to Americans with Alzheimer's cost the United States **$259 billion**.

The genes of mammals, such as chimpanzees, are similar to human genes.

PRO

Animal Testing is Accurate and Precise

Some people believe that researchers should create computer models or study human body cells instead of using animal testing. But these methods do not provide enough information. The bodies of humans and animals are made up of many organs, blood vessels, and nerves. All parts of the body system must work together. Each individual part is made up of cells. Each cell is more complicated than a computer program. In fact, these systems are too complex for computers to replicate. Studying body cells alone cannot show researchers how a disease or treatment affects the entire body.

Many animals have the same organs as humans. Their blood vessels and nerves are similar, too. Because their bodies are so similar, animals and humans often get the same diseases. Working with animals helps researchers understand how these diseases affect humans.

Ferrets are used in research about the heart, the brain, and the digestive system.

For example, the flu is an illness that causes a fever, weakness, and breathing problems in humans. The virus that causes the flu changes frequently. Therefore, scientists must develop new flu vaccines every year. Ferrets can also get the flu. They suffer from the same symptoms as humans. Studying ferrets that have the flu has helped scientists test and develop new flu vaccines. These vaccines can help prevent humans from getting sick.

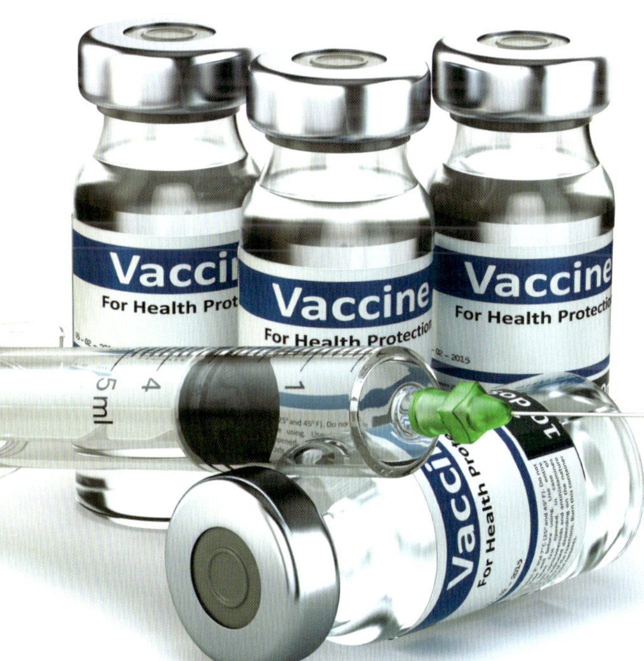

Each year, vaccines prevent between 2 and 3 million deaths worldwide.

Tuberculosis is another dangerous disease. In 2011, researchers used macaque monkeys to test a vaccine for the disease. Known as H56, this vaccine protected macaques that had been exposed to tuberculosis. The vaccine is currently being tested with humans.

About one third of monkeys in Asia are affected by tuberculosis. This is one of the reasons why they were used to test H56.

Transgenic Animals

Researchers alter the genes of some lab animals. One or more genes are transferred to the animal from another species. These animals, often mice, are called transgenic animals. They often have their genes changed to model a human disease. Work with transgenic mice has led to new drugs and treatments. These include ways to treat heart disease, diabetes, and cancer.

Even the genes of animals and humans are similar. Genes control much of how a living being looks and acts. Therefore, testing the reactions of animals is a good way to predict how humans might react. For example, mice have more than 95 percent of the same genes as humans. Mice are often used in cancer drug research. In a 2017 study, researchers gave a drug called *cabozantinib* to mice that had cancer. The drug caused their cancer to disappear. It is now being tested with humans.

Researchers can control the conditions in the labs where they do animal testing. Carefully monitoring the lab's temperature and light, as well as the animals' diet and health, helps researchers make sure their results will be as accurate as possible.

Rats and mice make up 95 percent of all lab animals.

Research labs must make sure their animals have adequate socialization.

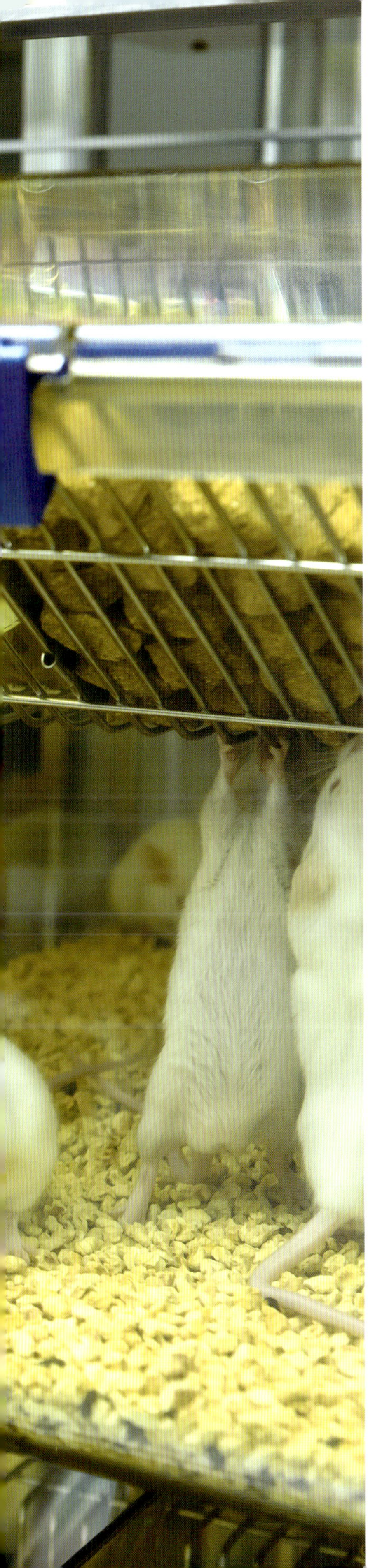

PRO

Laws Protect Research Animals

In the United States, federal and state laws protect the animals that are used for research. These laws help ensure the animals are properly cared for. According to the laws, lab animals must have clean housing and access to fresh air. Animals must also receive enough food and water. For example, the laws require labs to feed cats and dogs at least once a day. Cats and dogs must have access to water at least two times each day. The laws also give specific instructions for each type of animal. Cats must have access to clean litter. Dogs must have a place to exercise. Primates and marine mammals also have their own sets of rules.

Research labs must provide proper medical care for the animals. They are required to have a veterinarian who can **diagnose** and treat any diseases or injuries. In addition, lab staff must monitor the animals' health. They are required to observe each animal every day.

Each research lab also has a committee that inspects all its work with animals. This committee makes sure research labs follow the laws. Other inspectors examine each lab at least once a year. They check how the lab cares for, treats, and uses its animals. They also make sure the animals feel little or no pain and distress.

Additional guidelines for research labs were created in the 1950s. Known as the Three Rs, these guidelines stand for *replacement*, *reduction*, and *refinement*.

Laboratory animal veterinarians take care of the animals used in research labs.

Replacement guidelines urge researchers to use alternate methods whenever possible. For example, suppose a computer model of the heart can provide the same results as animal testing. The replacement guidelines ask researchers to use the model instead. Replacement guidelines also recommend using the simplest animal possible. For instance, mice are considered simpler than dogs. Therefore, researchers would try to use mice for testing instead of dogs.

Using simpler animals instead of more complex ones is an example of "relative replacement."

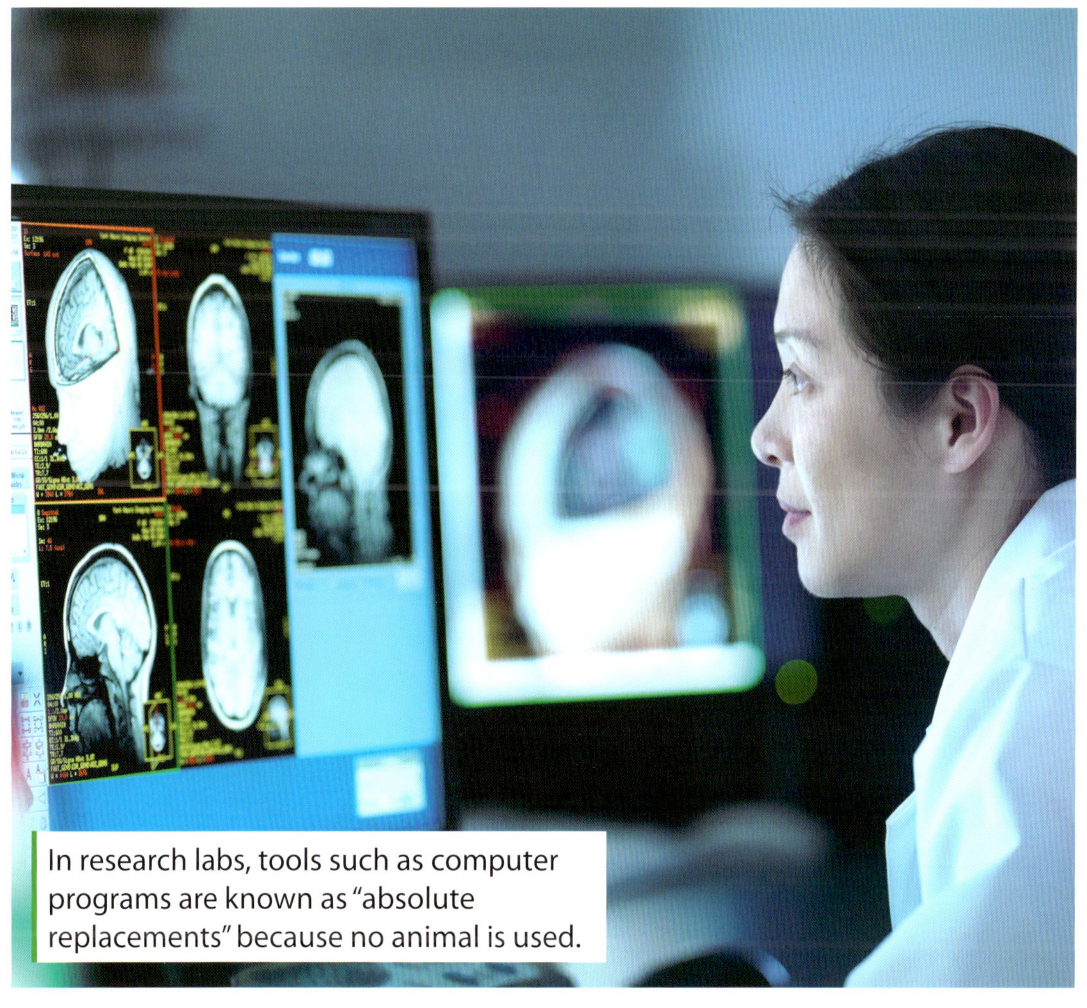

In research labs, tools such as computer programs are known as "absolute replacements" because no animal is used.

The reduction guidelines ask labs to use fewer animals when they conduct tests. Researchers design their tests to use the smallest possible number of animals. They also collect as much information as they can from each set of animals instead of running many tests.

The refinement guidelines aim to improve conditions for lab animals. This applies to all parts of the animals' care, not only the tests. Researchers make sure animals have adequate living situations. For example, mice are less stressed when they have comfortable and interesting housing.

Did You Know?

Animals that are less stressed tend to produce more accurate test results.

Comfortable housing for rodents includes access to water and places to hide.

Animal Testing Causes Animals to Suffer

Unfortunately, the animal protection system has many problems. Most animal protection laws do not include rats, mice, fish, and birds. These animals make up more than 90 percent of animals tested.

In addition, research labs usually choose the people who are part of their supervising group. As a result, group members may do what is best for the lab instead of what is best for the animals. Other lab inspectors must inspect large numbers of animals and test **procedures**. These inspectors may only visit most labs only once per year. For these reasons, it can be easy for them to miss many problems.

Lab animals are often crowded together in small cages.

Groups such as Cruelty Free International investigate animal research labs. These groups look at how the labs care for their animals and how researchers conduct their experiments. They have found many examples of animal suffering.

Research animals often live in poor conditions. In one lab, rabbit cages had no bedding to cover their floors. The cages hurt the rabbits' feet. Some rabbits died from their injuries. Other animals live in crowded cages and have little room to move. In other cases, they may be forced to live alone.

In addition, animals may be harmed during experiments. For instance, one lab used hundreds of monkeys for brain research. The monkeys spent their entire lives in cages. Researchers gave them brain damage as part of the study.

Animals may receive injections as part of the research.

On March 11, 2013, the European Union banned the use of animals to test cosmetic products.

Other tests may require animals to go without food or water. Sometimes animals receive food as a reward for learning new tasks. Before these tests, researchers may withhold the animals' food. They do so with the hope that hunger will motivate the animals to learn the tasks.

Researchers may also restrain the animals. An animal may be unable to move part or all of its body during the test. This can last for hours, days, or months. For example, monkeys were not given water for 22 hours as part of one research project. Then each monkey was placed in a restraining chair for an hour. Researchers gave the monkey vision tasks. They gave the monkey only one drop of water each time it performed a task.

In other tests, researchers give animals drugs or chemicals and observe how they respond. These tests are often painful. They may even be fatal. For instance, a test known as LD50 is used to determine how toxic a chemical is. In this test, animals are force-fed the chemical until half of them die. Researchers may even give animals diseases to test if new treatments are effective.

In 2013, the National Institutes of Health (NIH) in the United States announced that it would phase out research using chimpanzees.

Animal Suffering

Animals are affected in many ways by different kinds of tests. Some of these tastes may result in permanent injury or death.

Toxicity
Animals breathe, ingest, or are injected with a chemical, and researchers study how different amounts of the chemical affect the animal. This test often results in the death of the animals.

Eye Irritation
Animals have chemicals dropped into their eyes, and researchers study any irritation or injury that results. This test often results in redness, bleeding, or blindness.

Skin Irritation
Animals are shaved and have a chemical placed on their skin, and researchers study how it damages the animals' skin. This test often results in painful scabs, bleeding, or sores.

Reproductive Toxicity
Animals are given chemicals such as pesticides to see how these chemicals affect their ability to reproduce. This test often results in illness or death.

Developmental Toxicity
Animal embryos are examined to determine if or how the chemical affected their development. This test requires the death of both the pregnant animal and the embryos.

The drug penicillin causes vomiting in guinea pigs, but it is safe for humans to use.

CON

Animal Testing Does Not Predict Human Reactions

For years, researchers have used animals to test chemicals and medications. They assume that because animals are similar to humans, the results of the tests can predict how humans will react. However, each species' body is different. An animal will not respond to a treatment or drug the same way that a person would. As a result, testing drugs on animals can create results that do not apply to humans.

In addition, the animals live in research labs. The lab environment is highly controlled. This is much different from the regular world. Everyday life involves many more factors that can vary or change. Tests in a lab environment do not account for these factors. As a result, the tests cannot reliably predict what will work for people.

In fact, some drugs that did not work when tested on animals have been quite helpful for humans. For example, aspirin is a drug that can decrease pain, lower fevers, and reduce **inflammation**. But this valuable medicine failed terribly when researchers tested it on animals. Aspirin caused problems for mice, rats, dogs, and cats. When it was tested with humans, however, it proved to be safe.

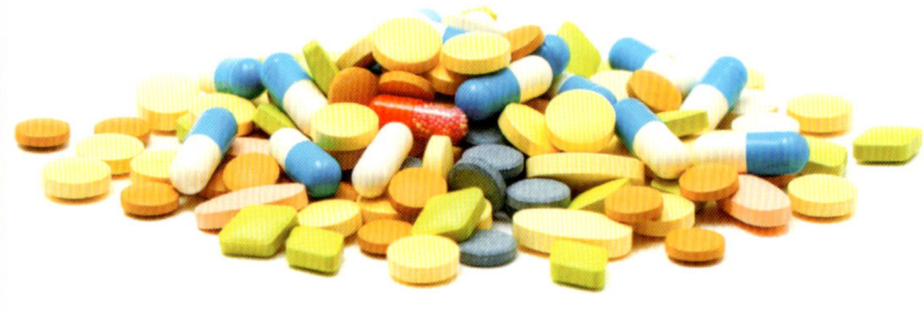

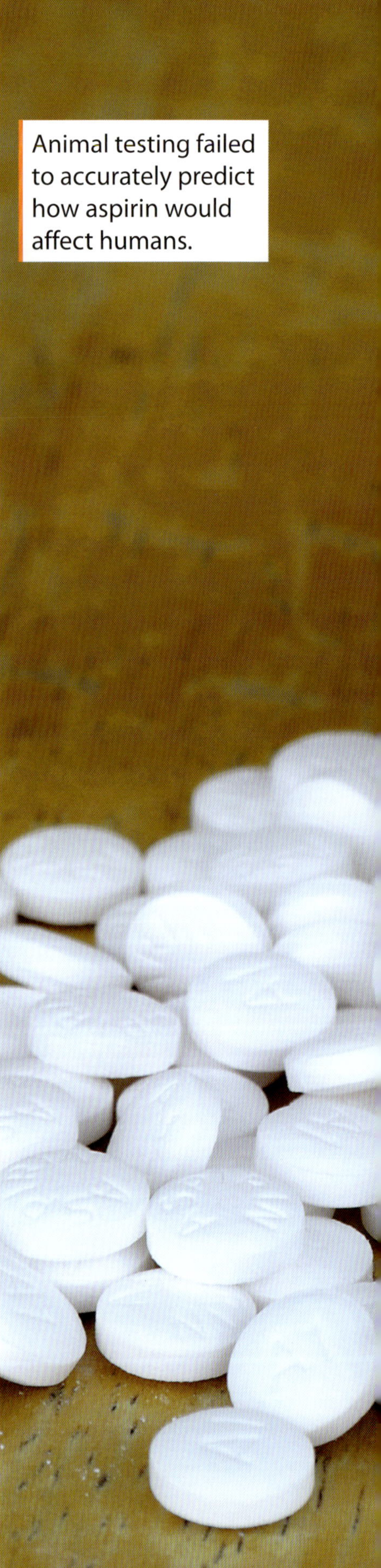

Animal testing failed to accurately predict how aspirin would affect humans.

Did You Know?

More than 80 vaccines for HIV worked when tested on chimpanzees but are not safe or effective for humans.

Many drugs in use today failed when they were tested on animals. Some of these drugs treat heart conditions or stomach problems. Others reduce pain. Some even fight infection or cancer. The differences between humans and animals may cause researchers to overlook drugs that could be helpful.

The opposite is also true. Drugs that pass animal tests can be harmful to humans. Some of these medicines can cause serious illnesses or heart problems. In some cases, drugs that pass animal testing can be fatal to humans.

For example, researchers tested a painkiller called Vioxx on several species of animals. The animals did not show any symptoms, so the drug was approved in 1999. But Vioxx caused serious illness and death in humans. The company that created Vioxx stopped selling the drug in 2004. By then, approximately 88,000 people in the United States had suffered from heart attacks after taking the drug. More than 35,000 of these people died.

Taking Vioxx doubled a person's risk of getting a heart attack or stroke.

The African green monkey, one animal used to test Vioxx, is often used for research about diseases and vaccines.

African green monkeys were introduced to the **Caribbean** in the **1600s**.

Cells from **one** African green monkey's **kidney** helped scientists develop vaccines for **polio** and **smallpox**.

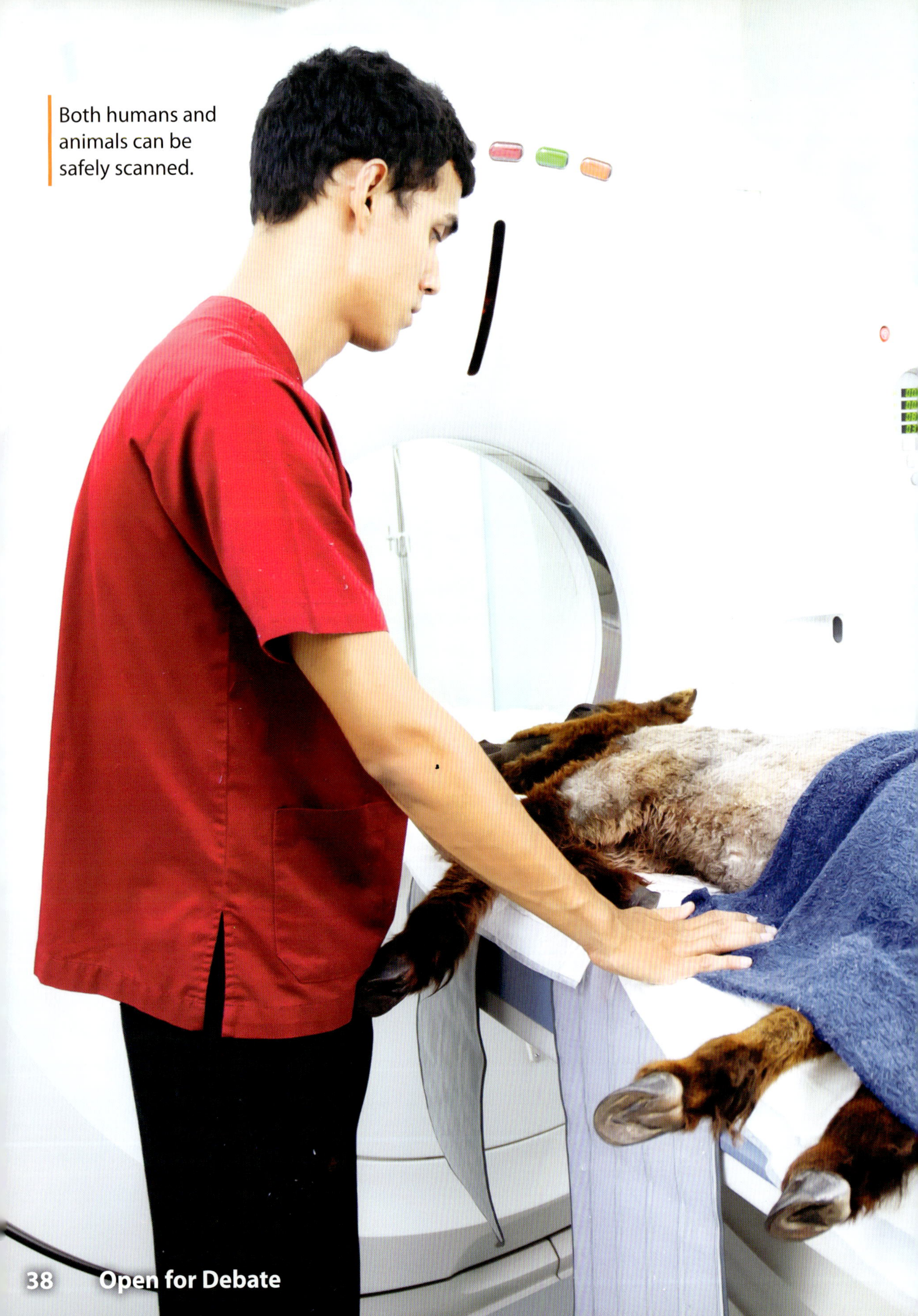

Both humans and animals can be safely scanned.

CON

Alternative Methods Provide Better Results

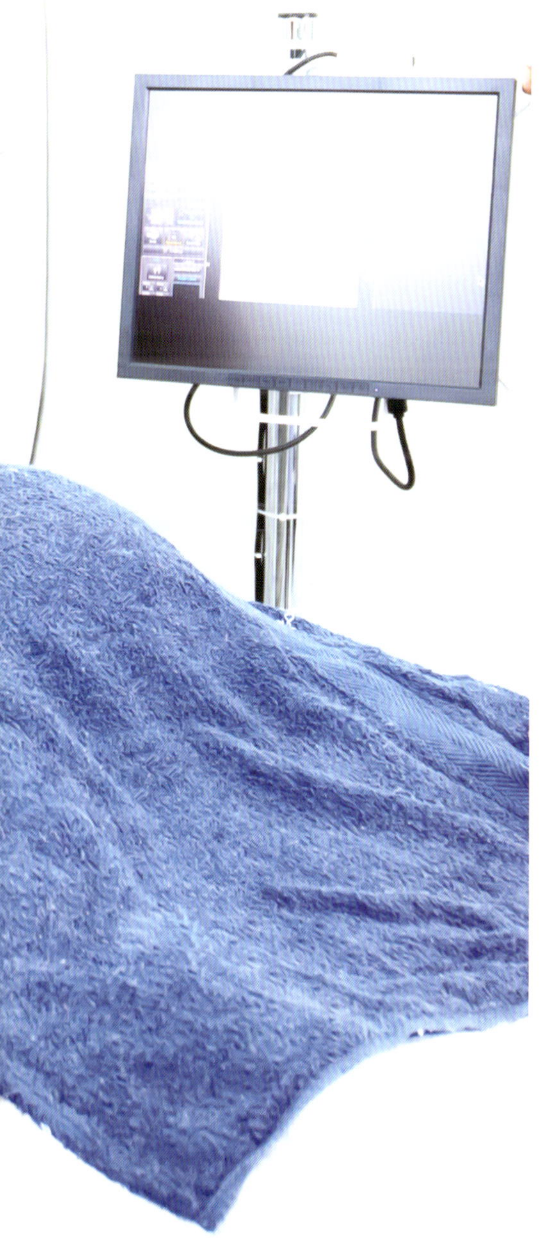

Today, researchers have many options for alternatives to animal testing. For instance, **MRI scans** can capture images of an animal's internal organs. Unlike surgery, the scans are painless. Plus, researchers can scan one animal multiple times instead of performing surgery on several animals. This reduces the number of animals needed for testing. MRI scans can even be used to study human organs and diseases.

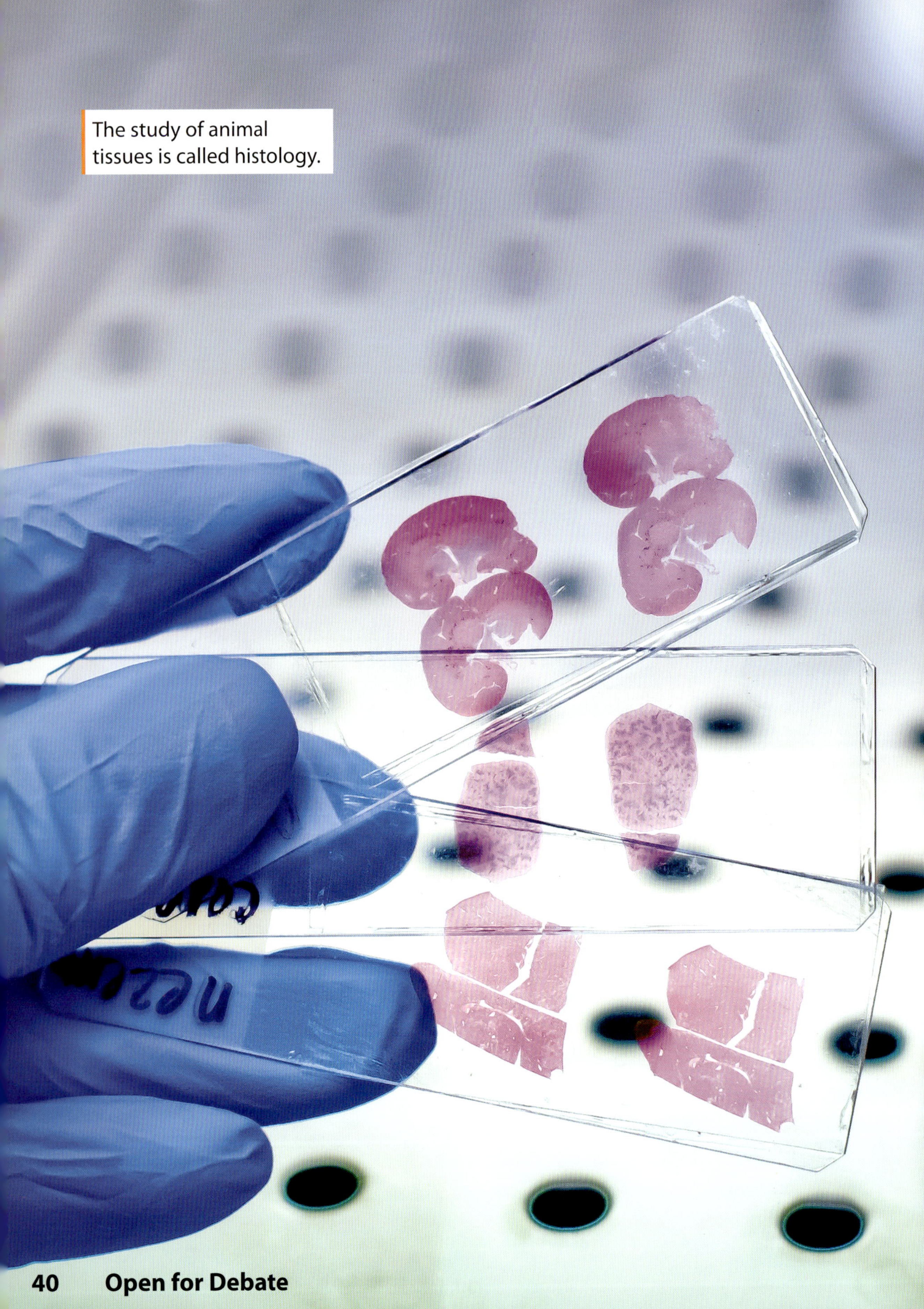

The study of animal tissues is called histology.

Other alternative methods can completely replace animal tests. The cell culture method allows researchers to study human cells instead of using animals. In this method, researchers collect samples of human cells or tissues. Then they grow the cells in test tubes in a research lab. Researchers study the cells as they grow to understand how the cells function. They can even use the cells to create models of diseases. This process allows researchers to test how the diseases would respond to different drugs or chemicals.

Researchers can also use computer **simulation** programs. The programs create models of human body systems and diseases. Researchers use the models to predict how new drugs will work in humans. For example, some computer programs test cancer drugs. The programs help predict how a patient's tumor will respond to a drug. This process helps doctors choose the best treatment for the patient.

Cell cultures can be used to create biological compounds such as vaccines.

Microdosing uses human volunteers to test new drugs. Volunteers receive tiny doses of the drug that are too small to cause a bad reaction. A highly sensitive device follows the path the drug takes through the body. It shows how the drug affects the body.

These alternative tests produce results without harming animals. They are often faster and less expensive than animal testing, too. Fewer people are needed to run the tests, and researchers do not need to house or care for animals.

Many alternative methods are based on human cells and organs. Because these methods work with models of the human body instead of animal bodies, the results tend to be more reliable. These methods provide an ethical and effective alternative to animal testing.

Organs-on-Chips

Organs-on-chips are one alternative to animal testing. To create them, researchers remove living cells from a human organ. They place the cells inside a small piece of clear plastic, or microchip. Studying the microchips helps researchers learn about the human body. For example, the lung-on-a-chip imitates the tiny air sacs in a lung. Researchers have also developed chips that mimic kidneys, skin, and intestines.

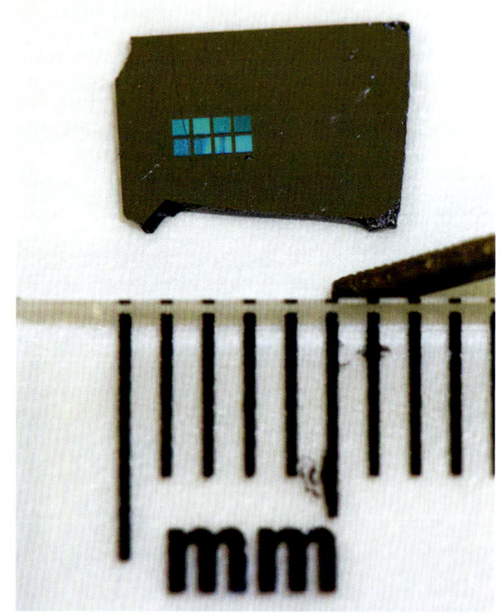

Preparing for a Debate

Many issues related to animal testing are controversial. People may feel very strongly about the topic. Consider the pros and cons carefully. Use what you have learned to help you prepare for a classroom debate.

1

What is the issue?

Are you for or against animal testing? Choose a position. It is important to enter into a discussion to hear all the points of view before making any decisions. Discussing or debating issues will make sure that the actions taken in the end are better for all involved.

2

Get the facts

Once you have chosen your position, research the topic. You can use sources including this book, the internet, and the library.

3

Use a concept web

A concept web can be a helpful research tool. Read the research questions in the concept web on this page. Use the relationships between concepts to help you understand your point of view.

Why did you take this position about animal testing?

How are people affected by animal testing? Who is impacted the most?

Should there be laws in your country relating to animal testing? Why or why not?

What historical events have impacted the debate about animal testing? How?

Animal Testing

Today, animal testing takes place all around the world. However, many companies, organizations, and governments are attempting to switch over to other testing methods that are just as accurate but do not require living subjects.

United States In 2000, an area of land in Keithville, Louisiana, was set aside as a home for retired laboratory chimpanzees. Today, more than 200 chimpanzees live in Chimp Haven.

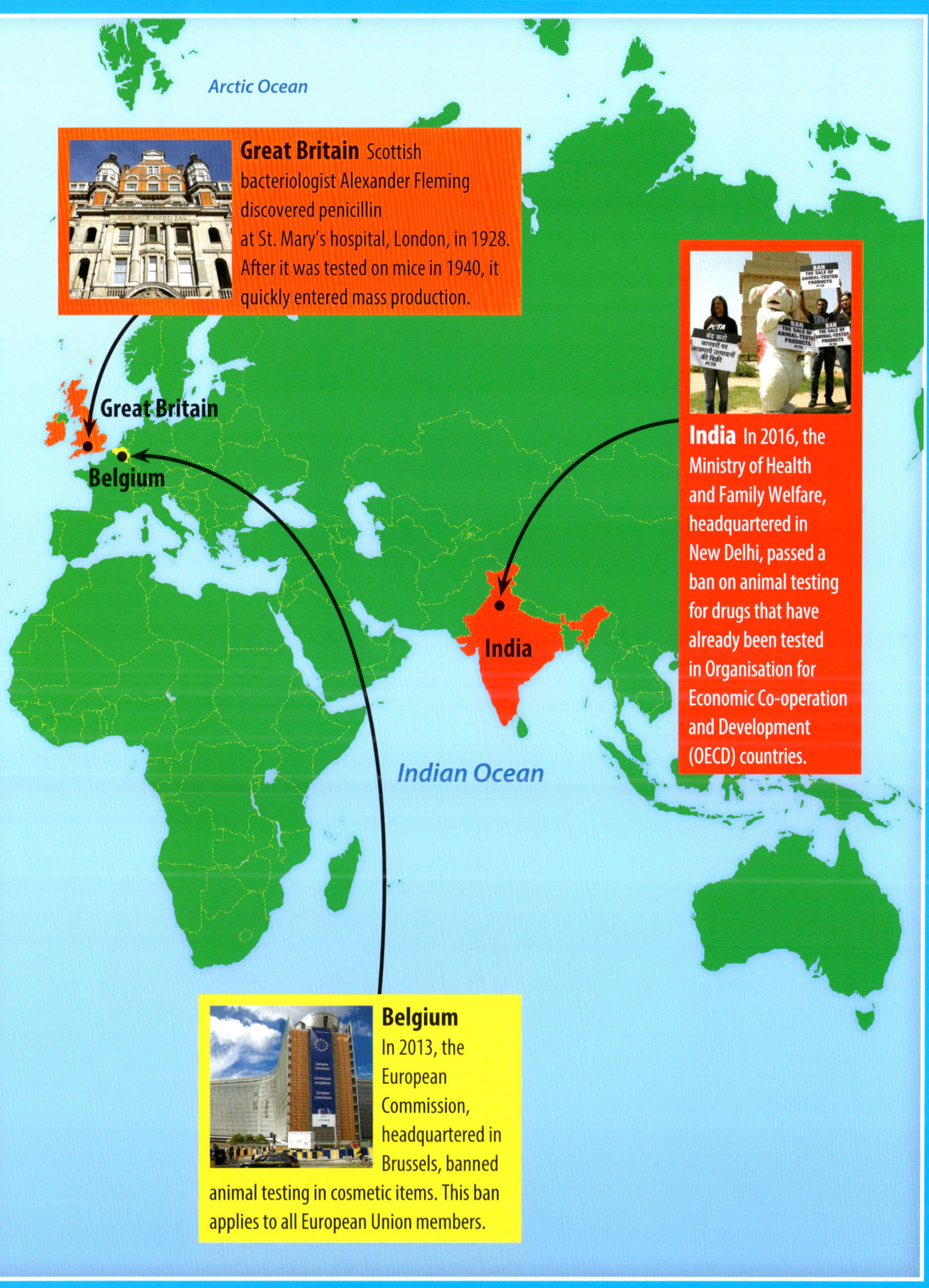
Arctic Ocean
Great Britain Scottish bacteriologist Alexander Fleming discovered penicillin at St. Mary's hospital, London, in 1928. After it was tested on mice in 1940, it quickly entered mass production.
India In 2016, the Ministry of Health and Family Welfare, headquartered in New Delhi, passed a ban on animal testing for drugs that have already been tested in Organisation for Economic Co-operation and Development (OECD) countries.
Great Britain
Belgium
India
Indian Ocean
Belgium In 2013, the European Commission, headquartered in Brussels, banned animal testing in cosmetic items. This ban applies to all European Union members.

Quiz

1

Which animals are not included in most animal protection laws?

2

Why do humans and other animals often get the same diseases?

3

What was the first U.S. state to ban cosmetics tested on animals?

4

Which painkiller was approved in 1999 but withdrawn because it could cause serious injury or death in humans?

5

What is the study of animal tissues called?

6

How has the cancer survival rate in the United States changed since 1970?

7

What are the Three Rs of animal testing?

8

When were the first pacemakers created?

ANSWERS **1.** Rats, mice, fish, and birds **2.** Because their bodies are relatively similar **3.** California **4.** Vioxx **5.** Histology **6.** It has doubled **7.** Replacement, reduction, and refinement **8.** The 1950s

Key Words

diagnose: to determine the disease that a person or animal has

genes: tiny parts of cells that tell the cells how to perform certain functions or cause the body to develop certain traits

glucose: a sugar found in plants that is converted to energy by the body

hypertension: an unhealthy level of high blood pressure

inflammation: heat, redness, and swelling that are part of the body's response to disease

MRI scans: procedures that use radio waves and a strong magnet to produce detailed images of the inside of the body

procedures: established ways or orders of doing something

simulation: something that is made to look or feel like something else

symptoms: signs of an illness or disease

transplants: surgeries in which an organ or other body part is removed from one person or animal and placed into the body of another person or animal

Index

LIGHTBOX

SUPPLEMENTARY RESOURCES

Click on the plus icon found in the bottom left corner of each spread to open additional teacher resources.

- Download and print the book's quizzes and activities
- Access curriculum correlations
- Explore additional web applications that enhance the Lightbox experience

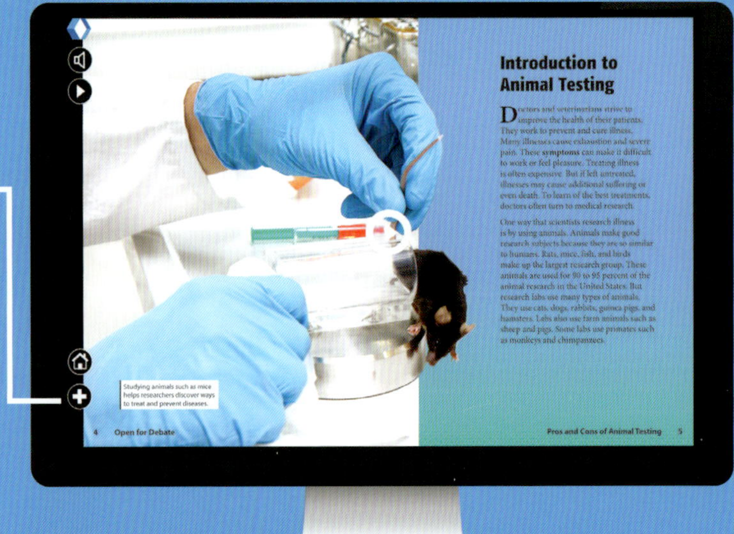

LIGHTBOX DIGITAL TITLES

Packed full of integrated media

VIDEOS

INTERACTIVE MAPS

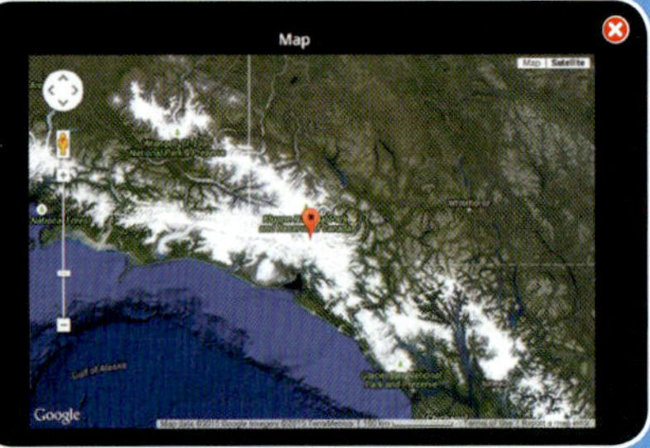

WEBLINKS

SLIDESHOWS

QUIZZES

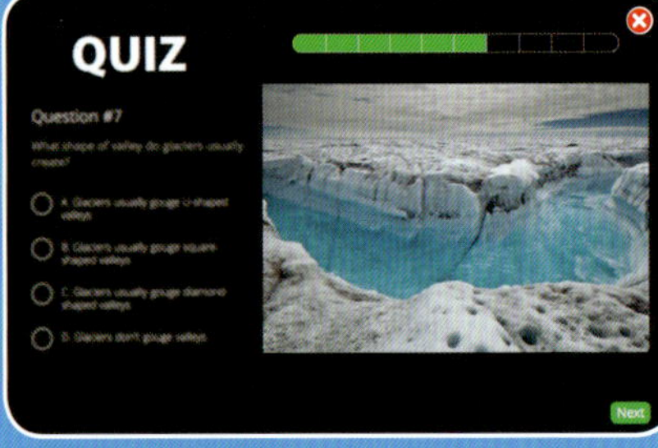

OPTIMIZED FOR

- ✓ TABLETS
- ✓ WHITEBOARDS
- ✓ COMPUTERS
- ✓ AND MUCH MORE!

Published by Smartbook Media Inc.
350 5th Avenue, 59th Floor New York, NY 10118
Website: www.openlightbox.com

Library of Congress Control Number: 2019939944

ISBN 978-1-5105-4765-0 (hardcover)
ISBN 978-1-5105-4766-7 (multi-user eBook)

Printed in Guangzhou, China
1 2 3 4 5 6 7 8 9 0 23 22 21 20 19

052019
121218

Project Coordinator: Priyanka Das
Art Director: Terry Paulhus

Photo Credits
Every reasonable effort has been made to trace ownership and to obtain permission to reprint copyright material. The publisher would be pleased to have any errors or omissions brought to its attention so that they may be corrected in subsequent printings. The publisher acknowledges Getty Images, iStock, Shutterstock, and Alamy as its primary image suppliers for this title.